Carolina Panthers

BY

ZACH WYNER

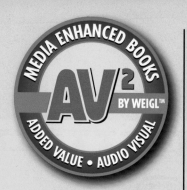

AV² provides enriched content that supplements and complements this book. Weigl's AV² books strive to create inspired learning and engage young minds in a total learning experience.

Your AV² Media Enhanced books come alive with...

Audio
Listen to sections of the book read aloud.

Key Words
Study vocabulary, and complete a matching word activity.

Video
Watch informative video clips.

Quizzes
Test your knowledge.

Go to **www.av2books.com**, and enter this book's unique code.

Embedded Weblinks
Gain additional information for research.

Slide Show
View images and captions, and prepare a presentation.

BOOK CODE

E 1 7 2 2 0 5

Try This!
Complete activities and hands-on experiments.

... and much, much more!

AV² by Weigl brings you media enhanced books that support active learning.

Published by AV² by Weigl
350 5th Avenue, 59th Floor
New York, NY 10118
Websites: www.av2books.com   www.weigl.com

Library of Congress Control Number: 2014930815

ISBN 978-1-4896-0798-0 (hardcover)
ISBN 978-1-4896-0800-0 (single-user ebook)
ISBN 978-1-4896-0801-7 (multi-user ebook)

Printed in the United States of America in Brainerd, Minnesota
2 3 4 5 6 7 8 9 0   19 18 17 16 15

022015
WEP050215

Project Coordinator Aaron Carr
Art Director Terry Paulhus

Photo Credits
Every reasonable effort has been made to trace ownership and to obtain permission to reprint copyright material. The publishers would be pleased to have any errors or omissions brought to their attention so that they may be corrected in subsequent printings.

Weigl acknowledges Getty Images as its primary image supplier for this title.

Carolina Panthers

CONTENTS

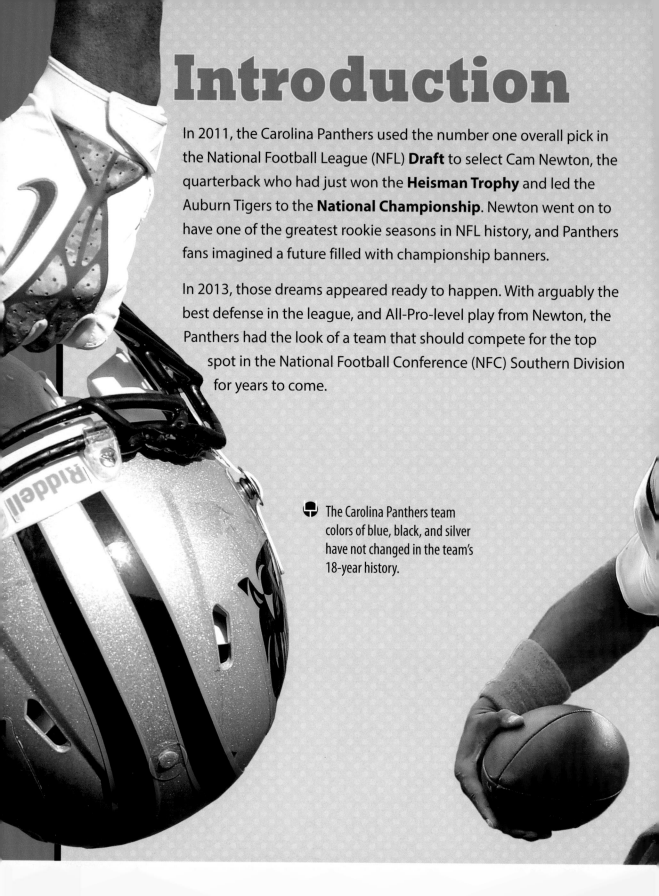

Introduction

In 2011, the Carolina Panthers used the number one overall pick in the National Football League (NFL) **Draft** to select Cam Newton, the quarterback who had just won the **Heisman Trophy** and led the Auburn Tigers to the **National Championship**. Newton went on to have one of the greatest rookie seasons in NFL history, and Panthers fans imagined a future filled with championship banners.

In 2013, those dreams appeared ready to happen. With arguably the best defense in the league, and All-Pro-level play from Newton, the Panthers had the look of a team that should compete for the top spot in the National Football Conference (NFC) Southern Division for years to come.

The Carolina Panthers team colors of blue, black, and silver have not changed in the team's 18-year history.

The city of Charlotte has long been a hub of the basketball world. With storied programs such as the University of North Carolina and Duke University close to the city, college hoops has been dominant for decades. However, with the surging Panthers racking up wins, the balance in Charlotte has begun to change.

Cam Newton is the current quarterback for the Panthers. He was drafted by Carolina in 2011.

CAROLINA PANTHERS

Stadium Bank of America Stadium

Division NFC South

Head Coach Ron Rivera

Location Charlotte, North Carolina

Super Bowl Titles None

Nicknames Cardiac Cats

5
Playoff Appearances

1
Conference Championship

4
Division Titles

History

NO DROUGHT

The Panthers have NEVER gone longer than ····· **6**YEARS without a playoff appearance.

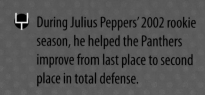 During Julius Peppers' 2002 rookie season, he helped the Panthers improve from last place to second place in total defense.

In just their second NFL season, the 1996 Carolina Panthers won the NFC Western Division. Head Coach Dom Capers was named Coach of the Year, and the team sent five defensive players to the **Pro Bowl**. They won their first playoff game, but fell in the NFC Championship Game. Soon after, the Panthers came down to earth. Veteran defenders lost a step, and with the offense in disarray, they moved further from the playoffs. The team hit rock bottom in 2001 when they finished the season with a 1-15 win-loss record.

In 2002, the Panthers switched divisions to the newly formed NFC South. One year later, head coach John Fox returned the team to glory. With Jake Delhomme starting at quarterback, third-year wide receiver Steve Smith registered his first of many 1,000-yard receiving seasons, and Pro Bowl running back Stephen Davis rushed for 1,444 yards. Just two years after going 1-15, the Panthers won the NFC South and advanced all the way to **Super Bowl** XXXVIII. They lost to New England in a thriller, 32-29.

In 2011, the Panthers reinvented themselves, hiring coach Ron Rivera and drafting Cam Newton. With one of the NFL's most dynamic players taking snaps for the foreseeable future, the most exciting moments in Panthers' history have yet to be written.

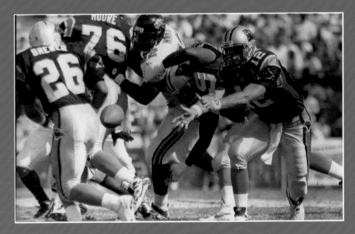

The Panthers finished 7-9 in their opening season, the best mark ever for a first-year team.

The Stadium

Bank of America Stadium seats 73,778 fans.

Bank of America Stadium enjoyed quite a debut in 1996, as the Carolina Panthers went 12-4 and won the NFC West. That season, the stadium also hosted its first playoff game, a 26-17 Carolina Panthers victory over the Dallas Cowboys. Also known as "The Vault," Bank of America Stadium is an open-air arena built on a 33-acre (13-hectare) plot of land in Charlotte, North Carolina. It was built specifically to house the Carolina Panthers. However, it also hosts a number of other events, including an **annual** college football game called the Belk Bowl, soccer matches, concerts and conventions.

The stadium is unique in that it was fully funded by the sale of Permanent Seat Licenses. Knowing that selling these seat licenses was the only way to build the stadium without using public funds, 40,000 football fans from North and South Carolina made purchases in a single day, enough to fund the entire stadium. Despite North Carolina's basketball bias, attendance at Carolina Panthers games has always been solid. In 2012, the Panthers ranked sixth in the NFL, with an average attendance of more than 73,000.

Though basketball may be the state's first love, you would not be able to tell by watching Panthers fans on Sundays.

Hungry Carolina football fans go to JJR's BBQ Shack to chow down on brisket and pulled pork sandwiches.

Where They Play

CANADA

Lake Superior

Washington
Oregon
Montana
North Dakota
Minnesota
Wisconsin
Idaho
South Dakota
Wyoming
Iowa
Illinois
Nevada
Nebraska
Utah
California
Colorado
Kansas
Missouri
UNITED STATES
Arizona
New Mexico
Oklahoma
Arkansas
Texas
Louisiana
Mississippi

30
29
15
16
32
14
13
23
22
24
31
17
12
27

Pacific Ocean

Alaska
0 500 Miles
0 500 km

Hawai'i
0 100 Miles
0 100 km

MEXICO

Gulf of Mexico

AMERICAN FOOTBALL CONFERENCE

EAST		NORTH		SOUTH		WEST	
1	Gillette Stadium	5	FirstEnergy Stadium	9	EverBank Field	13	Arrowhead Stadium
2	MetLife Stadium	6	Heinz Field	10	LP Field	14	Sports Authority Field at Mile High
3	Ralph Wilson Stadium	7	M&T Bank Stadium	11	Lucas Oil Stadium	15	O.co Coliseum
4	Sun Life Stadium	8	Paul Brown Stadium	12	NRG Stadium	16	Qualcomm Stadium

Bank of America Stadium

Location
800 South Mint Street
Charlotte, North Carolina

Broke ground
April 22, 1994

Completed
September 14, 1996

Surface
grass

Features
- high-definition monitors
- ribbon boards
- 158 executive suites

LEGEND
- American Football Conference
- National Football Conference
- Bank of America Stadium

NATIONAL FOOTBALL CONFERENCE

EAST	NORTH	SOUTH	WEST
17 AT&T Stadium	21 Ford Field	25 Bank of America Stadium	29 Levi's Stadium
18 FedExField	22 Lambeau Field	26 Georgia Dome	30 CenturyLink Field
19 Lincoln Financial Field	23 Mall of America Field	27 Mercedes-Benz Superdome	31 Edward Jones Dome
20 MetLife Stadium	24 Soldier Field	28 Raymond James Stadium	32 University of Phoenix Stadium

The Uniforms

SAME AS IT EVER WAS

Jerry Richardson, the Panthers' owner, claims that **NO** major uniform changes will be made during his lifetime.

The phrase "keep pounding" is on the collar of the Panthers' jerseys. The saying honors former Panther Sam Mills, who died in 2005 and lived by the motto to "keep pounding" rather than quit in his fight to beat cancer.

The Panthers' uniforms have remained largely unchanged since their beginning in 1995. The primary colors are white, black, and blue, with white and silver pants. The only detail that gave the owners pause was which shade of blue they should select. Rival basketball programs Duke University and the University of North Carolina both wore blue, and it was important that the Panthers not take sides. In the end, they decided upon "process blue," a shade lighter than Duke blue and a bit darker than North Carolina blue.

HOME

AWAY

While the Panthers' primary uniforms have undergone no significant changes, the team's all-black **alternate uniform**, worn with blue socks and silver helmets, won NFL.com's Greatest Uniform in NFL History contest.

Football uniforms have changed over time to become tougher and more elastic. This makes it easier for players to move quickly on the field.

The Helmets

1ST FOOTBALL HELMET

George Barclay made the

• **1st Football Helmet** •

from leather straps to protect his head and ears.

NFL helmet designs have changed over time to improve player safety. Older helmets were made from leather, while modern helmets are made from lightweight plastic shells.

Panthers' owner Jerry Richardson decided upon the name "Panthers" long before the city of Charlotte was awarded an **expansion team**. In fact, Richardson went as far as getting a **logo** designed two years before the Panthers took the field. The logo developed was nothing short of thrilling, and its fierce features have been on the sides of the Panthers' helmets from day one.

The Carolina Panthers' helmet is silver with two blue-bordered black stripes running down the center. On either side of the helmet is the now iconic logo of a fiercely growling panther, its mouth open wide, displaying long, sharp teeth. The panther's head is black with a blue border. It has white eyes, nose, whiskers, and teeth. Blue lines can be found on the panther's neck, and muscle is evident beneath its fur. The electrifying symbol instills excitement, awe, and fear in fans and foes alike.

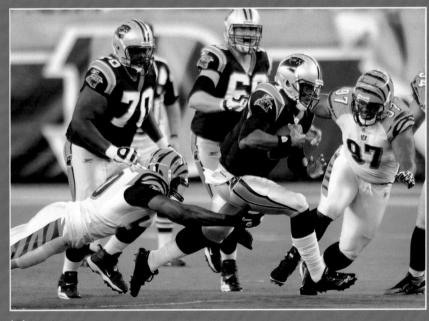

Football is a very physical sport. Helmets, as well as leg and shoulder pads, are required to keep players safe.

The Coaches

12 In Ron Rivera's third season in Carolina, he directed the team to 12 wins, a steady improvement from six, and then seven wins, in his two seasons prior.

Former Panthers coach John Fox is currently the head coach of the Denver Broncos.

In the short history of their franchise, the Carolina Panthers have been privileged to have some of football's greatest minds calling the shots from the sidelines. It is no accident that this team was able to accomplish so much so quickly, and it is no accident that they are now in the process of clawing their way back to the top.

DOM CAPERS

After 24 years as an assistant coach for college and professional teams, Dom Capers took the reins in Carolina. As the first coach of the expansion Panthers, Capers had some leeway. No one expected miracles. However, in the Panthers' second year, the conservative, defensive-minded Capers coached them to a division title and an NFC Championship Game appearance.

JOHN FOX

Like Capers, John Fox also spent 24 years as an assistant before getting his shot at the head coaching position with Carolina. In two seasons, Fox transformed the Panthers from a 1-15 train wreck into NFC Champions. His 73 regular season wins and eight playoff wins are the most in franchise history.

RON RIVERA

After two seasons with sub-**.500** finishes, the historically conservative Ron Rivera began taking more chances in 2013. His "calculated risk" approach paid off. The Panthers rebounded from a 0-2 start, and won seven of their next eight games.

The Mascot

Sir Purr's favorite book is "The Cat in the Hat" by Dr. Seuss.

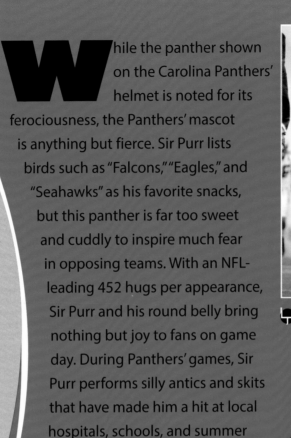

While the panther shown on the Carolina Panthers' helmet is noted for its ferociousness, the Panthers' mascot is anything but fierce. Sir Purr lists birds such as "Falcons," "Eagles," and "Seahawks" as his favorite snacks, but this panther is far too sweet and cuddly to inspire much fear in opposing teams. With an NFL-leading 452 hugs per appearance, Sir Purr and his round belly bring nothing but joy to fans on game day. During Panthers' games, Sir Purr performs silly antics and skits that have made him a hit at local hospitals, schools, and summer camps for years. Over the course of his celebrated career, Sir Purr has performed at the NFL Pro Bowl in Hawaii as well as the Celebrity Mascot Games in Florida.

Sir Purr loves *purr*-forming! He has made appearances at the Macy's Thanksgiving Day Parade in New York City, and even the Chinese New Year Parade in Hong Kong!

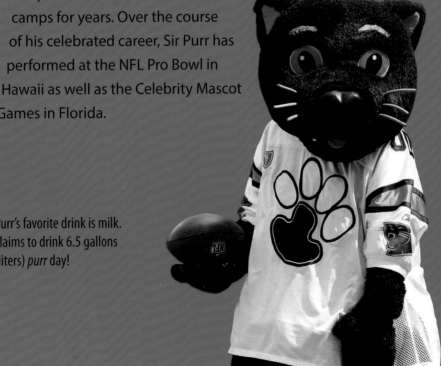

Sir Purr's favorite drink is milk. He claims to drink 6.5 gallons (25 liters) *purr* day!

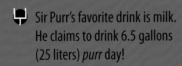

Legends of the Past

Many great players have suited up in the Panthers black and blue. A few of them have become icons of the team and the city it represents.

Kris Jenkins

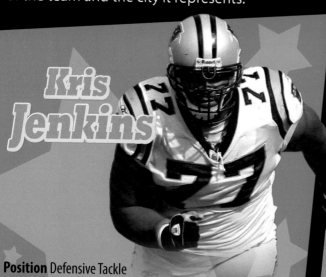

Position Defensive Tackle
Seasons 10 (2001–2010)
Born August 3, 1979, in Ypsilanti, Michigan

Every Super Bowl contender needs a large and powerful body to clog the middle and protect against the run. For the 2003 Carolina Panthers, this role was filled by 6-foot, 5-inch, 360-pound All-Pro Kris Jenkins. With both the ability to get into the **backfield** and the size to prevent the offensive line from creating holes through which opposing running backs might scamper, Jenkins was the immovable boulder in the middle of the Panthers' defense. In a 2003 game against the Tampa Bay Buccaneers, Jenkins blocked two kicks.

Jake Delhomme

In his first season with the Carolina Panthers, Jake Delhomme led them somewhere no one expected them to go, Super Bowl XXXVIII. Initially slated as the back-up quarterback to veteran Rodney Peete, Delhomme took over in the second half of the team's first game of the 2003 season. He erased a 17-0 halftime deficit with three second-half touchdown passes and promptly took over the starting job. That season, Delhomme engineered eight game-winning drives in the fourth quarter of overtime, the most in NFL history. In the Panthers' Super Bowl loss, he threw for 323 yards, three touchdowns and zero interceptions.

Position Quarterback
Seasons 15 (1997–2011)
Born January 10, 1975, in Breaux Bridge, Louisiana

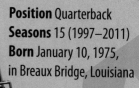

Steve Smith

n Steve Smith's first play as a professional, he returned the game's opening kickoff for a touchdown. While used occasionally as a receiver during his rookie campaign, it was not until 2002 that he established himself as an every-down receiver. In the Panthers' charmed 2003 season, Smith caught 88 passes for more than 1,000 yards. In 2005, he led the NFL in receptions (103), receiving yards (1,563), and receiving touchdowns (12). His efforts earned him the NFL's Comeback Player of the Year Award and solidified his role as the Panthers' most dangerous offensive weapon. Today, Smith is the franchise's all-time leader in total touchdowns, receptions, and receiving yards.

Position Wide Receiver
Seasons 13 (2001–2013)
Born May 12, 1979, in Carlsbad, California

Julius Peppers

uring his time with the Carolina Panthers, Julius Peppers established himself as one of the game's best defenders. The incredibly athletic and versatile lineman set the franchise-record for **sacks** with 81, intercepted six passes, returned two interceptions for touchdowns, forced 30 fumbles and deflected 46 passes.

Using terrific speed and his 6-foot 6-inch, 280-pound frame, Peppers had a rare ability to take over a game from the defensive side of the ball. Able to overpower offensive linemen or chase running backs from behind, Peppers was a near-unstoppable force. In eight seasons with the Panthers, he made five Pro Bowls and was named NFL's Defensive Player of the Year in 2004.

Position Defensive End
Seasons 12 (2002–2013)
Born January 18, 1980, in Wilson, North Carolina

Stars of Today

Today's Panthers team is made up of many young, talented players who have proven that they are among the best players in the league.

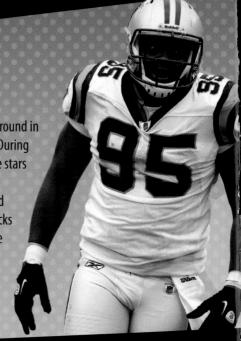

Charles Johnson

University of Georgia standout Charles Johnson somehow fell to the third round in the 2007 NFL Draft. The Carolina Panthers could not have been happier. During his first couple of years, Johnson showed great potential as a back up to defensive stars Julius Peppers and Mike Rucker. In 2010, he became the cornerstone of Carolina's **defensive line**. In his first full season as a starter, Johnson had 62 tackles and led the team with 11.5 sacks. During the 2012 season, Johnson set career highs in sacks (12.5) and forced fumbles (7), and in 2013, he surpassed the 10-sack mark for the third time in his career with 11 quarterback takedowns.

Position Defensive end
Seasons 7 (2010–2013)
Born May 12, 1987, in Honolulu, Hawaii

DeAngelo Williams

DeAngelo Williams played for a relatively small college football program at the University of Memphis, but as their star running back, he put up some huge numbers. In his four-year college career, Williams had 134 100-yard rushing games and rushed for 6,026 yards, fourth most in National Collegiate Athletic Association (NCAA) history. As a Carolina Panther, Williams has set many franchise records, including most rushing yards in a single season (1,515) and most rushing yards in a single game (210). Already the Panthers' record holder in career rushing yards and career rushing touchdowns, his grip on the Carolina record books gets stronger with each game.

Position Running Back
Seasons 8 (2006–2013)
Born April 25, 1983, in Little Rock, Arkansas

Luke Kuechly

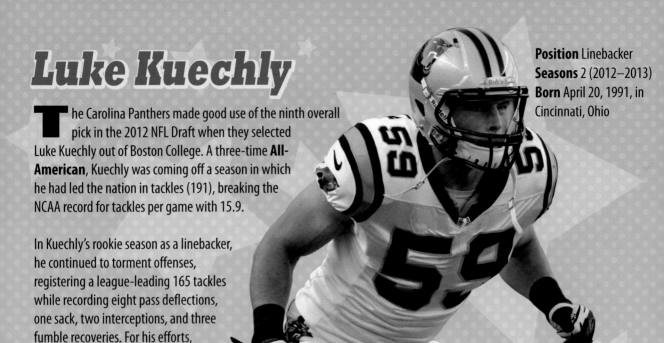

Position Linebacker
Seasons 2 (2012–2013)
Born April 20, 1991, in Cincinnati, Ohio

The Carolina Panthers made good use of the ninth overall pick in the 2012 NFL Draft when they selected Luke Kuechly out of Boston College. A three-time **All-American**, Kuechly was coming off a season in which he had led the nation in tackles (191), breaking the NCAA record for tackles per game with 15.9.

In Kuechly's rookie season as a linebacker, he continued to torment offenses, registering a league-leading 165 tackles while recording eight pass deflections, one sack, two interceptions, and three fumble recoveries. For his efforts, he was named Associated Press Defensive Rookie of the Year.

Cam Newton

Shortly after leading the Auburn Tigers to the National Championship and being awarded the Heisman Trophy, Cam Newton was selected with the first overall pick in the 2011 NFL Draft by the Carolina Panthers. Carolina fans did not have to wait long to see their team's investment pay off. In the first NFL game of his first NFL season, Newton broke the passing record for yards in a debut game (422). In his rookie season, he became the first rookie quarterback to pass for more than 4,000 yards and rush for more than 700. His 14 rushing touchdowns were more than any quarterback in NFL history.

Position Quarterback
Seasons 3 (2011–2013)
Born May 11, 1989, in Atlanta, Georgia

All-Time Records

81   Career Sacks

Julius Peppers is the Panthers' career sacks leader. His highest single-season total came in 2008 when he sacked opposing quarterbacks 14.5 times.

19,258   Career Passing Yards

The quarterback of the 2003 NFC Champion Panthers, Jake Delhomme amassed more passing yards than any quarterback in team history.

73 Coaching Wins

John Fox is the all-time leader in coaching wins with 73 over the course of nine seasons.

36 Single-Season Passing Touchdowns

With 36 touchdown passes, Pro Bowl quarterback Steve Beuerlein set the bar extremely high in 1999.

1,515 Single-Season Rushing Yards

DeAngelo Williams rushed for a Panthers' record 1,515 yards in 2008, averaging 5.5 yards per carry and scoring 18 touchdowns.

Timeline

Throughout the team's history, the Carolina Panthers have had many memorable events that have become defining moments for the team and its fans.

1993
The NFL announces that Carolina will be the home of the 29th NFL franchise. Owner Jerry Richardson publicly thanks more than 40,000 supporters who purchased Permanent Seat Licenses, funding a stadium to be built in Charlotte.

1995
In the Panthers' **inaugural** season, they play their home games at Clemson University. Led by **free agent** signees Don Beebe, Sam Mills, and John Kasay, the Panthers recover from a 0-5 start to finish the season with a respectable 7-9 record.

On January 5, 1997, in their first playoff game, the Panthers defeat the Dallas Cowboys, 26-17.

| 1992 | 1994 | 1996 | 1998 | 2000 | 2002 |

1996
Before the season begins, the Panthers pick up Steve Beuerlein, tight end Wesley Walls and linebacker Kevin Greene. The Panthers finish the season on a seven-game winning streak and win the NFC West.

1999
After two disappointing seasons, the Panthers hire new head coach George Seifert, replace quarterback Kerry Collins with Steve Beuerlein, and finish the season with an 8-8 record. Beuerlein passes for a Panthers'-record 4,436 yards but the team narrowly misses the playoffs.

2001
The team has a terrific draft in which they select three future All-Pro players, Steve Smith, Dan Morgan, and Kris Jenkins. However, during the season, the wheels come off. Following a Week One win against the Minnesota Vikings, the Panthers lose 15 straight games.

2002
Carolina hires John Fox to be their new head coach and drafts Julius Peppers from the University of North Carolina. Peppers, Mike Rucker, Brentson Buckner, and Kris Jenkins form one of the best defensive lines in the NFL and the Panthers improve to 7-9.

CAROLINA PANTHERS

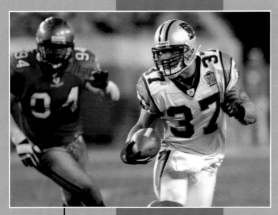

The Future

The future could not be brighter in Carolina. With an outstanding defense led by second-year linebacker Luke Kuechly, an offensive line anchored by center Ryan Kalil, and one of the most dynamic quarterbacks in the history of the NFL in Cam Newton, the Panthers can beat teams in a variety of ways. The franchise that shocked fans with their historically fast start will not be surprising anyone in the coming years.

2004
Steve Smith breaks his leg, Kris Jenkins is sidelined by shoulder problems, and the Panthers lose their top four running backs to injury. However, after a 1-7 start, fullback Nick Goings, wide receiver Muhsin Muhammad, and NFL Defensive Player of the Year Julius Peppers help the Panthers recover to finish 7-9.

> The Panthers select Cam Newton of the Auburn Tigers in the 2011 NFL Draft

| 2004 | 2006 | 2008 | 2010 | 2012 | 2014 |

2005
The Panthers rebound from their injury-plagued season, going 11-5 and making the playoffs as a wild card. Steve Smith emerges as a star, leading the league with 1,563 receiving yards, 103 receptions, and 12 touchdowns.

2010
Following a tough 2-14 season, Ron Rivera replaces John Fox as the Panthers' head coach.

2003
The Panthers rally around cancer-stricken former linebacker turned coach Sam Mills. Jake Delhomme, Stephen Davis, and Ricky Proehl bolster the offense and the Panthers make the playoffs.

2013
After a 1-3 start, Ron Rivera alters his offensive philosophy, deciding to take more chances on fourth down. The Panthers win six straight games, eventually claiming their division with a 12-4 record.

Write a Biography

Life Story

A person's life story can be the subject of a book. This kind of book is called a biography. Biographies often describe the lives of people who have achieved great success. These people may be alive today, or they may have lived many years ago. Reading a biography can help you learn more about a great person.

Get the Facts

Use this book, and research in the library and on the Internet, to find out more about your favorite Panther. Learn as much about this player as you can. What position does he play? What are his statistics in important categories? Has he set any records? Also, be sure to write down key events in the person's life. What was his childhood like? What has he accomplished off the field? Is there anything else that makes this person special or unusual?

Use the Concept Web

A concept web is a useful research tool. Read the questions in the concept web on the following page. Answer the questions in your notebook. Your answers will help you write a biography.

Concept Web

□

Adulthood
- Where does this individual currently reside?
- Does he or she have a family?

□

Your Opinion
- What did you learn from the books you read in your research?
- Would you suggest these books to others?
- Was anything missing from these books?

□

Childhood
- Where and when was this person born?
- Describe his or her parents, siblings, and friends.
- Did this person grow up in unusual circumstances?

□

Accomplishments off the Field
- What is this person's life's work?
- Has he or she received awards or recognition for accomplishments?
- How have this person's accomplishments served others?

Write a Biography

□

Help and Obstacles
- Did this individual have a positive attitude?
- Did he or she receive help from others?
- Did this person have a mentor?
- Did this person face any hardships?
- If so, how were the hardships overcome?

□

Accomplishments on the Field
- What records does this person hold?
- What key games and plays have defined his or her career?
- What are his or her stats in categories important to his or her position?

□

Work and Preparation
- What was this person's education?
- What was his or her work experience?
- How does this person work; what is the process he or she uses?

Trivia Time

Take this quiz to test your knowledge of the Carolina Panthers. The answers are printed upside-down under each question.

1 Which player is the Panthers' all-time leader in passing yards?

A. Jake Delhomme

2 In which season did the Panthers franchise first qualify for the playoffs?

A. Second

3 Which defensive lineman holds the Panthers' record for career sacks?

A. Julius Peppers

4 What is the name of the shade of blue chosen for the Panthers' uniforms?

A. Process Blue

5 Which Panther quarterback passed for more than 4,000 yards in his rookie season?

A. Cam Newton

6 Which Panthers' defender was named Associated Press Defensive Rookie of the Year in 2012?

A. Luke Kuechly

7 What is the fans' nickname for Bank of America Stadium?

A. The Vault

8 Where did the Carolina Panthers play their home games during their inaugural season?

A. Clemson University

9 What are Sir Purr's favorite snacks?

A. Falcons, Eagles, and Seahawks

10 How many division titles have the Panthers won?

A. Four

Key Words

.500: a season when a team wins and loses an equal number of games. In the NFL, an 8-8 record constitutes a .500 season

All-American: a player, usually in high school or college, judged to be the best in each position of a sport

alternate uniform: a uniform that sports teams may wear in games instead of their home or away uniforms

annual: something that occurs once a year

backfield: the area of play behind either the offensive or defensive line

defensive lines: defensive linemen line up directly on the line of scrimmage, close to the ball. There are two positions usually considered part of the defensive line: Defensive Tackle (DT) and Defensive End (DE)

Draft: an annual event where the NFL chooses college football players to be new team members

expansion team: a brand new team in a sports league, usually from a city that has not hosted a team in that league before

free agent: a player who is not currently under contract to play with a particular team

Heisman Trophy: an annual award given to the college football player who best demonstrates excellence and hard work

inaugural: marking the beginning of an institution, activity, or period of office

logo: a symbol that stands for a team or organization

National Championship: the top achievement for any sport or contest in a particular nation

Pro Bowl: the annual all-star game for NFL players, pitting the best players in the National Football Conference against the best players in the American Football Conference

sacks: a sack occurs when the quarterback is tackled behind the line of scrimmage before he can throw a forward pass

Super Bowl: the NFL's annual championship game between the winning team from the National Football Conference (NFC) and the winning team from the American Football Conference (AFC)

Index

Log on to www.av2books.com

AV² by Weigl brings you media enhanced books that support active learning. Go to www.av2books.com, and enter the special code found on page 2 of this book. You will gain access to enriched and enhanced content that supplements and complements this book. Content includes video, audio, weblinks, quizzes, a slide show, and activities.

AV² Online Navigation

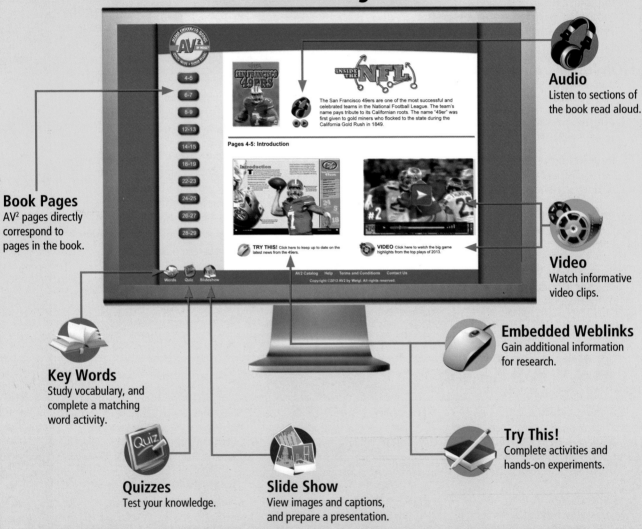

Book Pages
AV² pages directly correspond to pages in the book.

Audio
Listen to sections of the book read aloud.

Video
Watch informative video clips.

Embedded Weblinks
Gain additional information for research.

Key Words
Study vocabulary, and complete a matching word activity.

Try This!
Complete activities and hands-on experiments.

Quizzes
Test your knowledge.

Slide Show
View images and captions, and prepare a presentation.

AV² was built to bridge the gap between print and digital. We encourage you to tell us what you like and what you want to see in the future.

Sign up to be an AV² Ambassador at www.av2books.com/ambassador.